Y0-BYZ-088

Thurgood Marshall

by Jill C. Wheeler

visit us at
www.abdopub.com

Published by ABDO & Daughters, an imprint of ABDO
Publishing Company, 4940 Viking Drive, Suite 622, Edina,
Minnesota 55435. Copyright ©2003 by Abdo Consulting
Group, Inc. International copyrights reserved in all countries.
No part of this book may be reproduced in any form without
written permission from the publisher.

Printed in the United States.

Edited by Paul Joseph
Graphic Design: John Hamilton
Cover Design: Mighty Media
Interior Photos: AP/Photo, p. 22, 38, 43, 51, 55, 60
        Corbis, p. 1, 5, 6, 9, 10, 13, 15, 17, 19, 21, 25, 27, 29,
30, 33, 35, 37, 41, 45, 47, 49, 53, 57, 59, 61

Library of Congress Cataloging-in-Publication Data

Wheeler, Jill C., 1964-
    Thurgood Marshall / Jill C. Wheeler.
        p. cm. — (Breaking barriers)
        Includes index.
    Summary: Discusses the life of the first African-American to
serve as a judge on the United States Supreme Court.
    ISBN 1-57765-907-4
    1. Marshall, Thurgood, 1908-1993—Juvenile literature. 2.
Judges—United States—Biography—Juvenile literature. 3. African
American judges—Biography—Juvenile literature. 4. United States.
Supreme Court—Biography—Juvenile literature. [1. Marshall,
Thurgood, 1908-1993. 2. Lawyers. 3. Judges. 4. African Americans—
Biography.] I. Title.

KF8745.M34 W45 2003
347.73'2634—dc21
[B]

                                                2002074667

Contents

Leading the March

On February 3, 1999, government officials, journalists, and spectators gathered in Washington, D.C. They were there to visit a new traveling exhibit titled "Marching Toward Justice: The History of the 14th Amendment." The exhibit explored the experiences of African-Americans from the time of United States colonization through 1950.

It was fitting that the exhibit made its first stop at the Thurgood Marshall Federal Judiciary Center. Marshall had contributed more to the fight for civil rights than any other African-American lawyer in the twentieth century. Marshall's widow, Cecilia, was there to open the exhibit.

In his opening remarks, Wayne University president Irvin D. Reid spoke of Marshall as one of the true giants in African-American legal history. Marshall, he said, was "a man that, more than any other who has lived in this century, deserves credit for the legal victories achieved in the cause of civil rights."

Thurgood Marshall

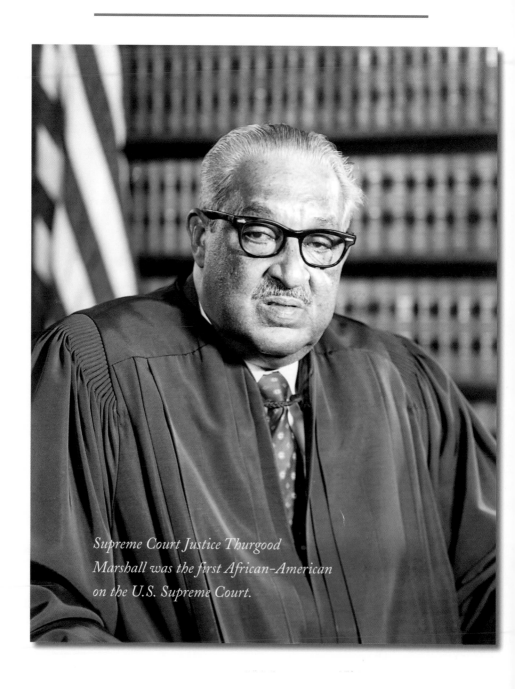

Supreme Court Justice Thurgood Marshall was the first African–American on the U.S. Supreme Court.

President Bill Clinton also spoke about Marshall at the opening. "We honor the courage of a man who traveled to the towns of the segregated South," Clinton said. "Places where he could not find a bite to eat when hungry, a bed to rest in when tired, or a police officer's protection when threatened." He did all that, Clinton added, to argue that we are all created equal.

Thurgood Marshall was a man who believed in the power of the law to effect change. Over the course of his career, he argued cases at the local, state, and federal levels, including the United States Supreme Court. His unwavering belief in equal justice through law eventually changed the course of American history.

Feisty Heritage

Thurgood Marshall was born on July 2, 1908, in Baltimore, Maryland. His parents were William and Norma Marshall. William worked as a waiter for the railroad. Later he worked as chief steward at an exclusive men's club. Norma stayed at home with Thurgood and his older brother Aubrey. She later went back to school and became a teacher.

Thurgood was named after his grandfather on his father's side. His grandfather was a freed slave who fought in the American Civil War. Prior to the war, he was known only as Marshall. When he joined the army, they told him he needed two names. He chose Thoroughgood for his first name. When young Thurgood was in second grade, he shortened his name from Thoroughgood. "I got tired of spelling all that," he said.

An African-American Union Infantry corporal holds an 1849 Colt pocket revolver during the Civil War.

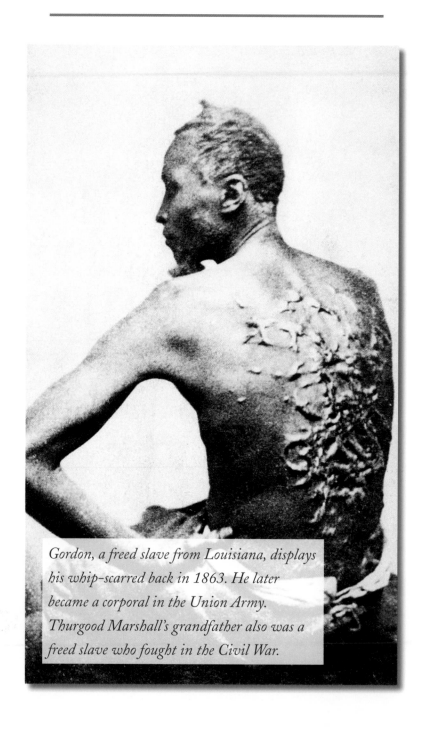

Gordon, a freed slave from Louisiana, displays his whip-scarred back in 1863. He later became a corporal in the Union Army. Thurgood Marshall's grandfather also was a freed slave who fought in the Civil War.

Thurgood loved stories. He had often heard stories about his mother's grandfather. Thurgood's great-grandfather had been captured from the African Congo and sold into slavery. He was mean and defiant to his owner. One day, his owner told him he didn't want to have to deal with him anymore. He said he didn't expect any other slave owner would want to either. So the owner set him free on one condition. Thurgood's great-grandfather was to leave the county forever.

Thurgood's great-grandfather accepted his freedom. But he didn't leave. He moved a few miles away from his former owner's farm and settled down. "He lived there until the day he died," Thurgood said. "And nobody ever laid a hand on him."

That was uncommon during those times. It was dangerous to be an African-American in the years following the Civil War. African-Americans could be, and often were, beaten just for saying something that offended a white person.

A Swing for Equality

T hurgood spent his youth on Druid Hill Avenue in Baltimore. "We lived on a respectable street," Thurgood said, "but behind us there were back alleys where the roughnecks and tough kids hung out." Thurgood enjoyed playing in the back alley with the tough kids. His brother, Aubrey, did not. "When it was time for dinner, my mother used to go to the front door and call my older brother," he recalled. "Then she'd go to the back door and call me."

Norma Marshall was a strong influence in Thurgood's life. She had high hopes for her boys and told them what she expected of them. She also encouraged them to focus on their education. Years later, she would sell her wedding ring to help pay for Thurgood's schooling.

Two inner-city youths play a game of basketball in a back alley.

As he grew, Thurgood faced the harsh reality of being black. His school was worse than the schools the white kids attended. His mother made less money than the white teachers. He also learned that some white people called African-Americans names, even if they were total strangers.

One of the worst names was "nigger." The first time Thurgood heard the word, he didn't know what it meant. He asked his father, and William explained it to him. William added, "Anyone calls you nigger, you not only got my permission to fight him—you got my orders to fight him."

That very thing happened when Thurgood was 15 years old. He had a part-time job working for a hat shop. One day, he was delivering some very expensive hats and had to take a trolley. Thurgood could barely see around the stack of hatboxes he carried. When he saw the trolley pull up, he blindly stepped toward it. Suddenly, a hand yanked him back. "Nigger, don't you push in front of no white lady again," a voice said.

Thurgood hadn't seen a white woman. Nor had he forgotten his father's orders. He took a swing at the white man who had pulled him back and insulted him. The two fought until a white police officer arrived.

Thurgood was arrested. But the white man wasn't even spoken to by the police. Thurgood called his boss, Mortimer Schoen, and told him what happened.

Schoen paid Thurgood's bail, told him he had done the right thing, and forgot about the ruined hats. Thurgood took pride in having stood up for himself in the face of prejudice.

Fifteen-year-old Johnny Gray points a warning finger at one of two white youths who tried to stop Gray and his sister from using the sidewalk on their way to school in Little Rock, Arkansas, in 1958.

Lawyer in Training

At the all-black Frederick Douglass High School, Thurgood played football and led the debate team. He earned a B average and also loved to socialize. Tall and handsome, young Thurgood was never at a loss for a date.

Thurgood sometimes got in trouble in high school. His punishment was to memorize parts of the U.S. Constitution. By the time he graduated from high school, he knew the entire document by heart.

One part of the Constitution really troubled him. The Fourteenth Amendment guarantees equal rights for all citizens. Yet Thurgood saw inequality all around him. He asked his father what the guarantee meant. His father said the Constitution specified how things should be. That didn't mean they were always that way.

Thurgood Marshall

William Marshall loved to talk about law. He had little formal education, yet he enjoyed arguing points of law with his sons. Often he spent free afternoons at the local courthouse. Sometimes he took his sons with him. "He never told me to become a lawyer," Thurgood recalled of his father. "But he turned me into one."

As 16-year-old Thurgood neared graduation, his mother wanted him to become a dentist. His brother Aubrey was already on his way to becoming a surgeon. But Thurgood was thinking of becoming a lawyer.

However, Thurgood's educational options were limited. Most northern colleges and universities would only admit a few blacks. Colleges and universities in the South would not admit blacks at all. Thurgood chose to go to the same college his brother attended. He went to Lincoln University in Oxford, Pennsylvania. He took some pre-med classes to please his mother.

Lincoln was limited to black men. But it was attended by students from around the world. About half of its graduates went on to graduate school. Thurgood would, too, but as a freshman that was the last thing on his mind.

Thurgood quickly formed the Weekend Club. The club was a group of students who swore they wouldn't be found on campus on the weekends. When on campus, he often played cards and had fun.

When not having fun, Thurgood found time to do a lot of reading. He poured through works by black writers and poets. He spent a lot of time thinking about the role of African-Americans in American society. And he began to think about how that role could be changed.

Segregated park benches

Beginning the Fight

Marshall and his college friends enjoyed going to movies. Marshall especially enjoyed Westerns. Yet even northern movie theaters were segregated. Usually African-Americans had to sit in the balcony, farther away from the screen. Some whites called the balconies "nigger heaven."

One day, Marshall and his friends put theater segregation to the test. They drove to the theater and bought their tickets as usual. But instead of going to the balcony, they sat on the main level of the theater. Soon a white man behind them spoke up. "Niggers," he said, "Why don't you just get out of here and sit where you belong?"

Marshall quietly told the man that he and his friends had paid for their tickets and intended to stay where they were. When an usher asked them to move, they refused. They sat through the entire movie on the main floor.

Police officers arrest a college student during a protest against racism.

Thurgood Marshall earned the nickname Wrathful Marshall for his debating skills.

Afterward, Marshall wrote to his parents about what had happened. He said none of the whites even looked at them as they were leaving. "I'm not sure I like being invisible," he wrote. "But maybe it's better than being put to shame and not able to respect yourself."

This incident and his father's influence led Marshall to dedicate his talents to improving civil rights. He was already bored with his pre-med classes. What inspired him and excited him was debate.

William Marshall taught his son how to argue well. Marshall had been on the debate team in high school. Now he joined the Lincoln debate club. He helped lead the team to many victories. He earned the nickname the Wrathful Marshall. This debate team experience would later help him become a lawyer.

Buster

Marshall and his friends sometimes went to Philadelphia on weekends. One weekend, they went to a social event at the Cherry Street Memorial Church. "We went there because we learned that's where all the cute chicks went," he admitted later.

He was not disappointed. He soon met a young woman named Vivian Burey. Burey, or Buster as she was called, was in her first year at the University of Pennsylvania. She was studying education.

After meeting Buster, Marshall stopped dating other women. He and Buster quickly fell in love and wanted to get married. "First we decided to get married five years after I graduated," Marshall recalled. "Then three, then one, and we finally did just before I started my last semester."

Marshall and Buster were married on September 4, 1929. Buster had graduated from college by that time, and Marshall had one semester left. The two moved into a tiny apartment, and Buster took a job as a secretary. Marshall worked as a bellhop and waiter to help pay their bills. The U.S. stock market crashed just months after the wedding. This plunged the nation into the Great Depression. Money became tighter than ever.

BLACK HERITAGE

A new commemorative postage stamp is unveiled in July 2002, honoring Thurgood Marshall.

Under Buster's influence, Marshall became a much better student. He graduated from Lincoln with honors in June 1930. By this time, he had given up pursuing a career in dentistry. He wanted to apply to the University of Maryland Law School in Baltimore.

The University of Maryland was an obvious choice. It had low tuition rates and was close to Marshall's home. However, it had not admitted an African-American student since the 1890s. Marshall was told that wouldn't change. So he never applied. Instead, he applied to Howard University Law School.

All his life, Marshall's race had determined which schools he could and could not attend. He believed that was wrong. He decided that someday he would do something about it. For now, though, he needed his law degree.

Marshall was accepted at the Howard University Law School in Washington, D.C. Howard accepted men and women of all races, yet most students were African-American. Marshall began classes in the fall of 1930. Within a week, he knew he was heading down the right path. It was a path toward justice.

An African–American studying law at Howard University in Washington, D.C., in 1942.

Social Engineering

Marshall's law school days were much different from his undergraduate days. Gone was the card-playing, socializing playboy. Now he and Buster lived with his parents to save money. Marshall was up by 5 A.M. every morning to catch the train to Washington, D.C. He caught another train when classes ended at 3 P.M. Then he headed to his part-time job. After working and having dinner with Buster and his parents, he hit the books. He often studied until midnight.

It was a brutal schedule, and it took its toll on Marshall. He went from weighing 170 pounds (77 kg) to just 130 pounds (59 kg). At the end of his first year, he was named the top student in his class. That honor earned him a job at Howard's law library. The job paid enough to keep him in law school. It also kept him in Washington, D.C., until 10 P.M. every night.

Thurgood Marshall

Charles Houston

Marshall quickly caught the eye of Howard University's professors. One in particular saw great promise in the young man. Charles Houston was vice-dean of the law school. He was also a talented attorney and civil rights activist.

In Marshall, Houston saw an outstanding candidate for what he called social engineering. Social engineering used law to fight injustice. It was a concept the Howard faculty had recently embraced. "Harvard was training people to join big law firms," Marshall explained later. "Howard was teaching lawyers to go to court."

Houston had been and continued to be involved with the National Association for the Advancement of Colored People (NAACP). He encouraged students to get involved as he and others in the law school helped plan NAACP cases. Marshall frequently joined in the late-night sessions. He impressed Houston and others with his intelligence and drive.

Howard demanded a lot from its law students. Marshall met every challenge. He graduated first in his class in 1933. Marshall then turned down a scholarship at Harvard Law School so he could begin practicing law right away. He successfully passed the bar exam, hired a secretary, and opened an office in Baltimore.

Freebie Lawyer

There weren't a lot of African-American attorneys in the United States in 1933. Most white people would not go to a black lawyer. Many black people felt they would get better treatment in court if they used a white lawyer. That was because judges and juries were usually white.

In 1933, few people had money to pay their lawyers. During his first year in practice, Marshall had no paying clients. He lost more than $3,000 that year. But he refused to send people away because they couldn't pay him. Marshall became known as the Freebie Lawyer. He used the freebie cases to polish his courtroom skills and make a name for himself. Eventually, he began getting paying clients.

One of his paying clients was involved in the local NAACP chapter. Marshall had been introduced to the NAACP early in his career. When the NAACP approached him, Marshall jumped at the chance to work there. He was happiest when working on civil rights cases.

Thurgood Marshall

One of his first NAACP cases was a boycott of Baltimore stores. The stores were happy to take money from black shoppers. However, they refused to hire black employees. The boycott led the stores to sue the NAACP. Marshall and his old teacher, Charles Houston, defended the organization in court. Amazingly, the white judge ruled in their favor.

The lawsuit was one of many Marshall would handle for the NAACP. The cases didn't earn him any money. The NAACP could only afford to pay his expenses. Yet Marshall was passionate about any case involving civil rights.

In 1935, Marshall approached Houston with a very special case. A young African-American man, Donald Murray, had applied to and been rejected by the University of Maryland Law School. Marshall asked Houston and the NAACP if they would help him and the young man take the case to court. They agreed.

In researching the case, Marshall looked to an 1896 ruling by the United States Supreme Court. The case was called *Plessy v. Ferguson*. The ruling said states could separate blacks and whites, provided each group had equal facilities. This practice became known as separate but equal.

Murray v. Pearson reached the court in June of 1935. It was Marshall's first major case. His parents and his wife were in the courtroom to show their support. With Houston as his counsel, Marshall argued that the state of Maryland had no law school for blacks. Therefore, there was no separate but equal facility. Hence, the school should be required to admit African-Americans.

The white judge agreed with Marshall. The University of Maryland admitted Donald Murray to its law school. And the victory made history. It also made Marshall very happy. He had finally defeated the law school that felt it was too good for African-American students.

Thurgood Marshall, standing, prepares the desegregation case against the University of Maryland in 1935.

Dangerous Game

Following *Murray*, Marshall worked on other education issues. He also helped black teachers in Maryland get pay closer to what white teachers received. But the country was still in the Great Depression. And he and Buster continued to struggle just to pay their bills.

In 1936, Marshall approached the NAACP and asked for a job. He was hired to work as the NAACP's assistant special counsel. He worked assisting Charles Houston. It was the number two legal job within the organization and paid $2,400 a year. It would be hard work. And it would mean traveling throughout the South, where black men could be killed for no reason at all.

Marshall began immediately. At first he divided his time between his office in Baltimore and NAACP headquarters in New York City. He continued working with his clients until he could transfer them to new attorneys.

Thurgood Marshall

Ku Klux Klan members at a cross-burning ceremony near South Bend, Indiana.

For the next 25 years, Marshall fought segregation laws. He and Houston focused on education issues. But at the same time, Marshall helped on other issues. He defended blacks unjustly accused of crimes. He also helped blacks vote in local elections, serve on juries, and find housing.

When Marshall came to town, the black community usually knew about it. Word of his arrival spread quickly. African-Americans viewed Marshall as someone who could help them. His strategies and arguments often did.

Marshall and Houston put in many hours. They traveled thousands of miles and saw hundreds of people. They typed legal briefs long into the night in their old, beat-up car.

These were dangerous times for Marshall. Most of his cases were tried in courtrooms in small southern towns. Racial prejudice was strongest in those towns. Many of them had active Ku Klux Klan (KKK) members. KKK members, or Klansmen, didn't hesitate to use violence to stop blacks from voting or holding office.

Marshall had to be careful not to stir up trouble when he traveled in the South. He ate at black restaurants and used black restrooms. He could not stay at white-owned hotels, so he stayed with African-American families. He would always change where he stayed after just one night so no one could predict his movements. Sometimes, he changed cars in the middle of his trip to throw off anyone who might be following him.

One night, Marshall almost lost his life. He was in Tennessee to defend two black men who had been arrested following a riot. On his way out of town, he was stopped twice and eventually arrested by a group of white police officers. They charged him with drunk driving and took him to a local judge.

They ordered him to walk alone to the judge's office. Marshall refused. He had heard of blacks being shot in the back in just such a situation. The officers would claim the African-American had been trying to escape. Marshall forced the officers to go with him to the office. The judge could tell Marshall hadn't been drinking. So he released him.

When Marshall was released, he had a second car drive in the opposite direction. Marshall escaped safely. The white officers were angry that their plan had been thwarted. They followed the wrong car and took their rage out on the wrong man when they caught him. The man was beaten so badly he had to be hospitalized for a week.

Marshall always respected the African-Americans who had to live in such conditions. "I go into these places and I come out, on the fastest vehicle moving," he said later. "The brave blacks are the ones who have to live there after I leave."

Thurgood Marshall, left, during a trial in Ocala, Florida, in 1952.

Helping the "Little Joes"

Charles Houston retired from the NAACP in 1938. In 1940, the NAACP established its Legal Defense and Educational Fund (LDF). LDF provided legal assistance to blacks who suffered because of prejudice. Marshall was appointed director-counsel of LDF. He took LDF's clients and their problems very seriously. He called his clients the "Little Joes."

LDF's cases sometimes involved forced confessions. It wasn't unusual in those days for police to beat and isolate black prisoners until they confessed to a crime. Marshall worked on two forced confession cases that went to the United States Supreme Court. The Court overturned the conviction on one but not the other. It was Marshall's first Supreme Court defeat. Throughout his career, he argued 32 cases before the nation's highest court. He lost four.

Another area of focus for LDF was voting rights. Southern states were skilled at keeping blacks from voting. They used poll taxes, literacy tests, and other restrictions. The restrictions usually worked.

*Thurgood Marshall in his
New York residence in 1962.*

In 1941, Marshall began work on a voting rights case involving a man named Lonnie Smith. The Democratic Party in Texas had denied Smith the right to vote in the primary election. Marshall took the case to the Supreme Court and won. Now blacks could not be denied the right to vote in any election, or in any state.

Following World War II, Marshall and the NAACP again attacked the South's Jim Crow laws. These laws and practices of segregation were intended to keep black people from achieving equality. Jim Crow was the name of an early Negro minstrel show.

Marshall's next victory came in a Supreme Court ruling that banned segregation on interstate buses. He also attacked housing policies that restricted where African-Americans could live.

In the late 1940s, Marshall again focused on higher education. Thousands of African-Americans had bravely served during World War II. These veterans were eligible for financial assistance from the government for education. Yet few schools would accept them. There was one school each in the entire south where blacks could study law, medicine, and pharmacy. There were no graduate engineering schools for blacks in the South at all.

An African-American pilot talks with his flight crew during World War II.

Marshall and the NAACP battled cases involving blacks seeking admission to graduate schools in Texas and Oklahoma. In both instances, the schools had set up low-quality separate programs for black students. Marshall argued that the separate schools were not equal. He went on to say that they never could be. He argued that keeping black students separate made those students feel inferior to white students. Hence, they could never be equal.

In both cases, the Supreme Court ruled in favor of the students. However, they did not strike down the separate but equal precedent. Marshall would have to wait for another case to do that. In 1952, he got that chance.

Segregation Showdown

Southern elementary schools had always been segregated. One such case was in Clarendon County, South Carolina. In 1951, the South Carolina NAACP found a group of black parents who agreed to sue in order to integrate the schools. Marshall went to South Carolina to argue their case.

Clarendon County had 276 white children. There was one teacher for every 28 students. Their two brick schoolhouses each had flush toilets, lunchrooms, and school buses. Meanwhile, the county had 808 black children. There was only one teacher for every 47 students. Their schools were three run-down, wooden buildings with outhouses and no lunchrooms. And the black children had to walk up to five miles (eight km) to get to school.

Marshall believed separate but equal schools were bad for black children. Now, he had to prove it to the court. He argued that segregated schools were unconstitutional. By segregating schools, black children were made to feel they were inferior to whites. As long as they felt this way, there could be no equal education.

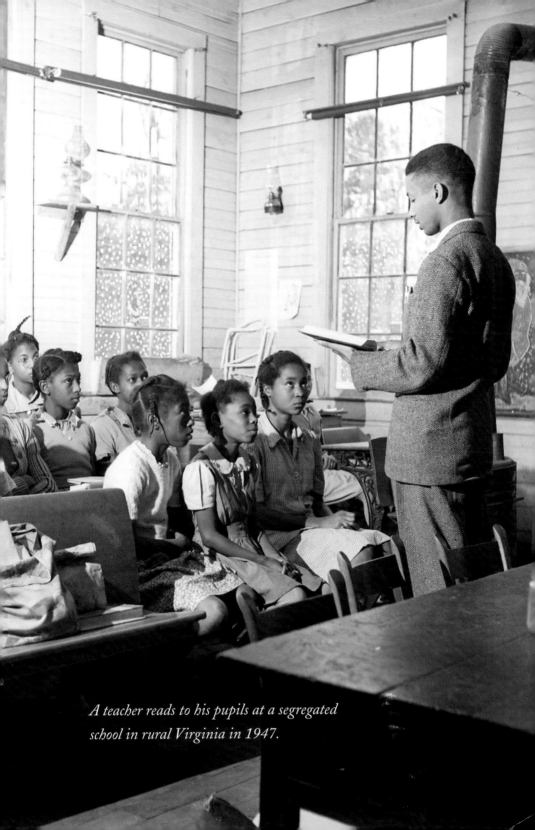

A teacher reads to his pupils at a segregated school in rural Virginia in 1947.

To prove his point, Marshall brought in psychologists and experts who had done tests on children in segregated schools. The tests showed that black children felt they were "bad" compared to white children.

Despite this evidence, the court ruled against Marshall. Some people criticized him for seeking to overturn the separate but equal principle. They felt if the schools truly were equal, segregation wouldn't be so bad. Marshall insisted that Southern states would never create equal schools for blacks if they continued to be segregated. He wanted to have the case heard by the United States Supreme Court.

The Court agreed to hear not only the South Carolina case, but also four other school segregation cases. They were lumped together under the name of a case from Kansas, *Brown v. Board of Education of Topeka*. Each case involved black parents suing to get better schools for their children.

Marshall knew it was the most important case of his career. He also knew he had a strong opponent. John W. Davis was representing the state of South Carolina. Davis was a leading constitutional lawyer. He had argued 139 cases before the Supreme Court. In college, Marshall had cut class to see him in action, and he knew Davis was good.

Marshall worked 23 hours a day preparing for the court date. He got advice from the best lawyers he knew. And he practiced his arguments until he knew them by heart.

Thurgood Marshall in front of the U.S. Supreme Court.

Landmark Ruling

Opening statements in *Brown* began on December 9, 1952. Marshall and his team presented their case before a packed courtroom. The justices listened intently and often interrupted with questions. Arguments in the five cases took three full days.

After they were done, Marshall worried about what the courts would do. The following June, the justices said they needed more information to make a decision. They provided Marshall and Davis with a list of five questions. And in the fall of 1953, Marshall had another opportunity to argue the case before the nation's highest court.

In the meantime, there had been a shift on the Court. Chief Justice Fred Vinson had died of a heart attack. President Dwight Eisenhower nominated Earl Warren as the new chief justice. Warren was instrumental in urging the justices to decide to end segregation in public schools.

The decision was handed down on May 17, 1954. It sent shockwaves through the nation. School segregation was ruled unconstitutional. This ruling sent Marshall into a state of elation. "I was so happy I was numb," he recalled.

Marshall's happiness over the ruling was short lived. In November 1954, Buster told him she was dying of lung cancer. She had known for a while but didn't want to distract him from the case. Marshall put his work aside and spent as much time as he could with his wife. When Buster died in February 1955, Marshall said, "I thought the end of the world had come."

Thurgood Marshall, center, with his team of lawyers, led the fight before the U.S. Supreme Court to abolish segregation in public schools.

On the Bench

Before *Brown*, Marshall was a celebrity to African-Americans. He was the most requested speaker at NAACP events and was on the front page of black newspapers every week. Following *Brown*, Marshall was a national celebrity. He was featured in white and black newspapers. African-Americans around the nation began calling him Mr. Civil Rights.

Meanwhile, the struggle for civil rights continued. In December of 1955, in Montgomery, Alabama, a black seamstress named Rosa Parks refused to give up her seat on the bus to a white person. Her brave act began a boycott of buses by African-Americans in Montgomery. The boycott lasted longer than a year. Marshall filed a lawsuit to desegregate the city's bus system.

Marshall won the case when it went to the Supreme Court. This meant blacks could sit anywhere they wanted on the bus. Parks's action had started this change. It also led to a new leader in the civil rights movement. He was Reverend Dr. Martin Luther King, Jr.

Rosa Parks sat in the front of a Montgomery, Alabama, bus on December 21, 1956. On this day a U.S. Supreme Court ruling took effect banning segregation on the city's public transit vehicles.

King and Marshall had similar goals. Yet they approached them very differently. Marshall believed he could create change by following the law. King believed unjust laws wouldn't be changed unless people refused to obey them. Throughout their lives, King and Marshall would have differences of opinion. Yet both made giant strides toward achieving civil rights for African-Americans.

In late 1955, Marshall had married a woman who had worked at the NAACP offices. Her name was Cecilia, or Cissy. By 1958, Thurgood and Cissy had two sons, Thurgood Jr. and John. Marshall enjoyed his time with them and started to spend less time on the road.

In 1960, Americans elected John F. Kennedy as president. He supported civil rights legislation. In 1961, President Kennedy nominated Marshall to serve on the United States Court of Appeals for the Second Circuit.

Marshall's nomination was confirmed, and he spent four years on the bench for the court of appeals in New York. He wrote more than 100 opinions, or rulings, during that time. None was ever reversed on appeal.

Solicitor General Thurgood Marshall stands behind President Lyndon B. Johnson at the White House in 1967.

A Justice for All

In 1965, President Lyndon B. Johnson appointed Marshall the U.S. solicitor general. The solicitor general is the main lawyer for the U.S. government. Some felt it would be Marshall's last stop before he was nominated to serve on the United States Supreme Court.

In June of 1967, there was an opening on the Court. President Johnson once told Marshall he wouldn't nominate him to the Supreme Court. Johnson told him so again. But then, Marshall was told to stop by the White House. President Johnson had reconsidered. He nominated Marshall on June 13, 1967.

Several Senators were opposed to Marshall's nomination. But the Senate accepted him in August of 1967. Marshall was publicly sworn in as a justice on the United States Supreme Court on October 2, 1967. Cissy, Thurgood Jr., John, and Marshall's brother, Aubrey, were in the audience. Marshall became the first African-American to serve on the Supreme Court.

On October 2, 1967, Thurgood Marshall
was sworn in as the first African-American
member of the U.S. Supreme Court.

Many of the cases Marshall heard still concerned desegregation in schools. As a justice, Marshall found a new way to tackle that issue. He was also able to work on other causes in which he passionately believed. He became known as a champion of individual rights.

Throughout his 24 years on the Supreme Court, Marshall fought for the "Little Joes." He opposed the death penalty because most death-row inmates were poor people and people of color. He also viewed the death penalty as cruel and unusual punishment and therefore unconstitutional.

As the years passed, the Supreme Court became more conservative. Marshall found that his opinions were often in the minority. He wrote many dissenting opinions. A dissenting opinion from a Supreme Court justice does not change the ruling of the court. However, it offers a justice a chance to say why he or she disagrees.

Despite his many dissents, Marshall was a popular and respected member of the Court. Throughout his life, he had an ability to relate to all types of people. He could fit in with the "Little Joes" at the local barbershop. Or he could impress the nation's top lawyers with his powerful arguments. He could be gruff and angry or easy-going and happy.

Colleagues recalled how he sometimes greeted Chief Justice Warren Burger with "What's shakin', chiefy baby?"

Marshall announced his retirement from the Supreme Court in June 1991. When asked why, he responded in his typical style. "I'm old," he said. "I'm getting old and falling apart."

Marshall left all of his personal papers to the Library of Congress. This meant his opinions would live on in use and study by journalists and scholars. Thurgood Marshall died on January 24, 1993, but his advances in civil rights will be seen forever.

The 1988 U.S. Supreme Court. Front row, left to right: Thurgood Marshall; William Brennan; Chief Justice William Rehnquist; Byron White; Harry Blackmun; Back row, left to right: Antonin Scalia; John Paul Stevens; Sandra Day O'Connor; Anthony Kennedy.

Timeline

July 2, 1908: Thurgood Marshall is born in Baltimore, Maryland.

1930: Marshall graduates with honors from Lincoln University.

1933: Marshall receives his law degree from Howard University and begins private practice in Baltimore.

1934: Marshall begins work for the Baltimore branch of the NAACP.

1935: Marshall and Charles Houston win the first major civil rights case, *Murray v. Pearson*.

1940: Marshall wins his first of 29 Supreme Court victories.

1954: Marshall wins *Brown v. Board of Education of Topeka*.

1961: Marshall is appointed circuit judge.

1965: Marshall is appointed U.S. solicitor general.

1967: Marshall becomes the first African-American to serve on the U.S. Supreme Court.

1991: Marshall retires from the Supreme Court.

January 24, 1993: Marshall dies at age 84.

Web Sites

Would you like to learn more about Thurgood Marshall? Please visit **www.abdopub.com** to find up-to-date Web site links about Thurgood Marshall and the U.S. Supreme Court. These links are routinely monitored and updated to provide the most current information available.

Thurgood Marshall

Glossary

boycott

To refrain from having any dealings with something, such as to refuse to buy anything produced by a particular company.

brief

A detailed summary of a legal argument.

civil rights

Rights found in the U.S. Constitution that are guaranteed to all American citizens.

discrimination

To treat some people better or worse than others because of their race, religion, gender, or some other factor.

dissenting opinion

A document written by a justice on the "losing" side.

Great Depression
The worst and longest economic collapse in the history of the industrial world.

Ku Klux Klan
An organization that works to keep blacks from voting or holding political office.

National Association for the Advancement of Colored People (NAACP)
An organization founded in 1909 for the purposes of improving the conditions under which African-Americans lived.

precedent
An example or rule that is used to justify the same action at a later time.

segregated
When races are kept separate from one another.

United States Constitution
The written document that outlines the basis of the government of the United States.

Index